FINDING WINGS

POEMS

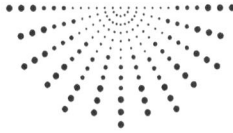

MICHELLE MORACZEWSKI

HOMESTEAD
PRODUCTIONS

.

Homestead Productions

ISBN -978-0-9861-496-1-0
Cover designed by Michelle Moraczewski
Illustrations by Michelle Moraczewski

Printed in the United States of America

For my Family

FINDING WINGS
P o e m s

1

CONTENTS

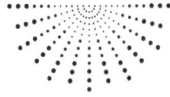

❧

❧

❧

PART I
TRIBUTE TO LOVE

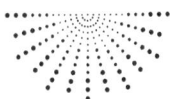

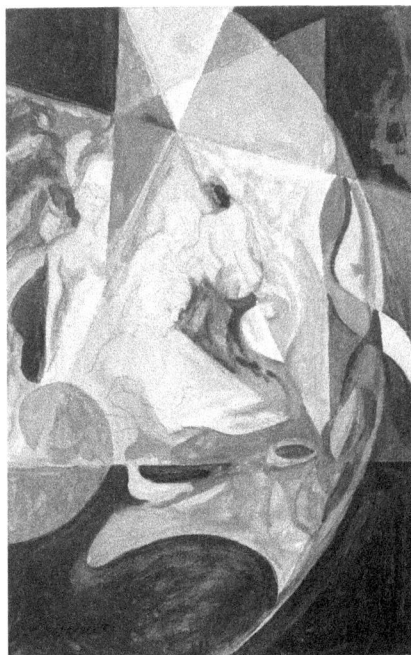

BEAUTIFUL HEART

The beauty of the day
Makes me change all my plans to leave,
I will stay.
As the light shimmers just past my door
I long to join it to my soul.
I run to the top of the hill.
Headed for a spot, a rock, a ledge, a hope,
for time to stand still,

to stretch the seconds of the sun's
Graceful fall into the purple hills beyond.
Clouds know I'm watching as they begin
Painting the sky like a dance,
Sending sunrays into pinks and orange and
lemon light.
While purple clouds touch purple hills
And the maple gleams magic
Sparklers in its leaves.

I know I was born a child of God
And God made this earthly garden
As a temporary Paradise.
With plums on my lips like kisses
And berries bursting in perfect ripeness
Between my teeth,
The deep warm moist musk
Of being one for a time with you.

Once the sun has set,
Only the moon watches over us.
Spread eagle on the blanket on the hill,
I know I cling to Earth.
All she gives and offers each day
For those who take the time
To stop and be.
Grounded barefoot on the hill.

While the sun goes down
And the moon comes up
Like this is the first day…
On the First day,
God created Day and Night.
And on the seventh day,
He rested.

2

VENICE

Venice is a world of beauty and story.
I got to know it best
on the fishermen's side of town.
Catching pieces of sunlight on fabric
Hung on a wash line
Stretched across narrow streets.

Light on the water reflected
On curved stone bridges
That arched over boats tied to the quay.
Inside St. Marks, dark as night
Yet aglow with gold reliquaries
Splintering back candlelight from within.

We lost each other on St. Mark's Square.
The fault was mine as I
Was staring too long at Mosaic designs
And the stained-glass mysteries inside.

I searched the square for your face.

The multitudes and hordes,
Children and tourists, saints, and sinners.
I walked around the covered colonnades.
I searched the back alleyways.
Lost on streets full
Of carnival masks and Jesters, laughing at my loss.

We found each other in the rain.
When everyone ran for cover.
The whole square was bare.
Except for the two of us, laughing in the center.

3

SUNRISE

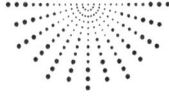

He, wrapped in white sheets, and sunrise.
Long and lean in the king size futon.
Thrown on the floor in front of big windows.
With a view of New York below.
Ambulances screech deep into the night.
A quiet comes with a sun-streaked dawn.
New York memories of fall escapades.

To the Catskills
Driving out for seafood
And stopping at a roadside Motel.
Out to Montauk
To the top of the lighthouse.
We watch the Atlantic soften the rocks below.
Lobster by the side of the road.
Sunrise entangled in sheets like memories

Mixed up and sweet.
Watching the endless sunset
When driving west

Across mountains from Virginia to Tennessee.
The adventure of together
Is like the trips we used to take.
The horizon always arriving
Over the next hill.

4

NIGHT

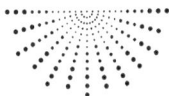

The smell of wine like blood
Assaulted my nostrils as I tossed and twisted
In a dream filled sleep
of a still dark morning.

Blood full and thick
Pulsed through the veins of my heart and hands.
Wine from the night before glowed red
in half empty crystal goblets

By a tormented fire.
Wind rattled the panes,
The maple creaked
While the big house stood firm

Alone in the wooded valley.
Dreams of death, murder, and betrayal
Abuse my sleep.
Confusion between work and home,
good and evil

Weave in an out of my consciousness,
Like the warp of the loom held taught
While rich strands of wool and alpaca
Twist and turn into the tapestry of life.

The mysterious tension between
dream and memory
In the battle between night and day
The sun and the moon,
Midnight and the golden dawn

The dark and the light.
The knower and the known lay still.
A woven tangle of shared imaginings.
the boundary between you and me is blurred.

Let me tell you my dream I say.
But that was my dream you say.

PART II
INSPIRED BY NATURE

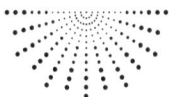

2
DARK

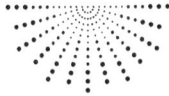

The light from above
surrounded by black sky
is caught in the dark wine glass like a diamond.

OVER YONDER

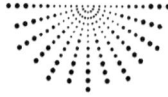

Paying attention to night sounds
while the cold air keeps us captive on the porch.

The insistent moo nearby
calls from the darkness.
A distant moo responds
from over yonder way.

As we listen to the bovine conversation,
the imagination can invent a story
or even devise a cow play.

I think it may be just as valid
as what we might miss on TV.

RIVER TRIO

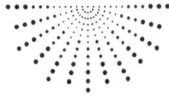

The green flat lake of water
Was not entirely still.
As I sat in the boat it kept moving
With no effort of my own.
The Dark water seemed so
In this quiet shadow of the cliff.

We were at a wide part of the river.
The few gold leaves
Fell upon the surface
And moved like small boats
Quickly along with froth and bits of moss.

I marveled at the cool darkness
As I stared at the surface.
The landscape changed
From cliffs to wooded bank
Little sun shone on this quiet
Forgotten bit of water.

Later as I stared at the still, mirror surface
I marveled as the piece of sky and clouds,
Like a V breaking the green velvet of the water.
I was ensconced in the white clouds,
Full of cotton fluff with smears of pink dashed upon them,
I watched them move and change by some unseen force.
I was surrounded by the unseen.
Forces of still water that pulled us forward,
Whether I rowed or not.
And the force that moved the fluff white clouds
Into shapes, and piles that were kingdoms
All their own upon the surface.

5
RIVER MYSTERY

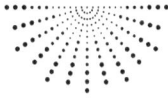

The route of the river is a mystery.
I float along paddling hard.
My canoe glides noiselessly
Upon the surface.
I stare hard at the water
Too mesmerized to paddle
I have become fascinated by
The bold reflected world
That lies so vividly before me.

My back begins to burn with the sharp heat of summer.
Sun sculpts the clouds.
I break the water to dip my hand
beneath the surface.
I spread the cool silver liquid
upon my brown strong legs,
my arms and shoulders.
But still I cannot see beneath
The plane of water
into that other world that lies below.

I stare at green velvet dark water
Knowing this river of my reality
Is awesome in its cold depth.
The river of my imagination sparkles
Like diamonds and shimmering laughing over rocks
And splintered stone.

This river is quiet and hushed.
Still in a way that draws me in. I stop falling.
I stop paddling
I let the river take me at her speed.
Show me what she will.
The big flap of the blue heron
Catches my concentration
My eyes follow the rise into the distance.
As she bends around a far hill.
Silver maples sparkle and bend towards the water,
Leaves catch the light.

I gaze into the face of this dark ancient river god.
Catch the sight of stones, shells and alabaster
That beckon from below.
But I am pulled out to the calm surface
Of cloud and sky
Reflected on her face.
Still waters run deep or
Deep rivers run slowly.
Or shallow streams glitter and dance
Like me.
Like my happy personality
That tickles and giggles and shimmers
With wine droplets on my full lips
Silver bracelets on my wrist.

Will this hidden depth of past

Secrets and mystery
Ever elude me
As my attention is so easily caught by light
And the silver slice
Of sunshine on the wing?

THE SHADE

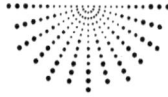

The shade.
The shade.
The shade.
I heard his voice beckon me
From this over bright southern sun.

It is a wet heat.
Water is wrenched from my pores
And saturates my skin
And the very clothes I wear
And my breath of air.

The southern summer
That can make you sleep in the afternoon
And crawl out from the shaded house
Come evening.
Ice cubes clink
In that wonderful Jack Daniels bourbon
That sits so cool and sweet upon your tongue.

The southern heat
That makes you slow and crave the relaxed life,
Of spiked lemonade and quiet neighbors.

The shade is a plant.
A dark nightshade that induces Hallucinations
And inspires thoughts
Of other worlds far
From the slow slugging thickness
Of sun dripping with honey laced bourbon,
Or coke gone flat.

How I struggle slitting my eyes open
A mere crack on the bright day.
While water sweat runs in rivulets
Tingling down my spine.

Let me be a true Southern son,
And learn to love this green world.
Green from my perch in the treetops
With distant green hills hiding
neighbors and the back woods folk.

We never lay our eyes on them.
Just the yelp
Of their half-wolf dogs when the coyotes holler
Across the meadow.
And of course the traps
Hidden in the broken stumps
of weather ruined trees.

LEAF BELOW THE THORN

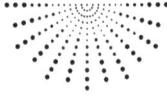

Poetry is the language of the soul.
My soul -Your soul - His soul.
It's our souls who understand
The beauty of the Word,.
The harmony of a rhyme
that makes no sense,
but creates a peace and generosity
of golden moments where time holds still.

To watch the dew
on the rose at dawn.
An entire sun held captive within the prism
of the drop before it moves,
to form and fall,
like a timeless sphere on
to the leaf below the thorn.

8
BLUE DAY

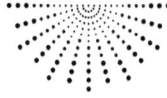

I gaze out at a beautiful day.
The cobalt blue etches around gold leaves
hung from black branches.

A bird sits upon my chair.
Like me hoping the breeze grows into a wind
that will blow some purple pregnant clouds our way.
So the rain can bless the earth
with her tears.

Instead the leaves dance down
to the brown barren pile below.
Dried and crusty before their time.

SOUTHERN FALL

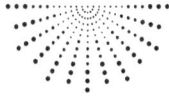

Cantaloupe colored trees
line the winding road
on my way to town.
A few pale rubies frame the straw faded
grasses on the hills waiting for water.

Fall in Tennessee is Latin
In its color hue usually.
This world of rivers without rain
has become strange
a surreal blue.

The air smells like burning leaves
the smoke floats in from afar
it lies trapped in valleys between buxom hills.

The smoke mixes with the spirit mists
trapped so long ago.
Many lost in the Civil War

floated home on mists
and still remain.

An honorable retreat.

PERSIMMON HILL

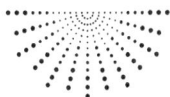

The Sun chases the Moon around the earth.
We picked persimmons on the hill
I lay on a blanket, watching the small
fruit fall
like rain upon the cloth.

I picked thru the orange plunder,
My fingers sticky-sweet.
He kissed me then.
Staking a claim
We felt like homesteaders again.
On persimmon hill
Watching the moon rise sun fall.

LAST COLOR

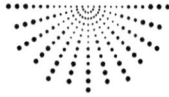

Reds , ruby, pink, cumquat, peach,
Siena, gold.
All on one tree.
Surrounded by a world gone brown.
Tawny brown and smoky grey.
As fall makes the turn towards
colder times.
I still cling to color.

WEATHERING STORMS

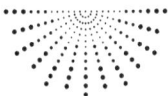

The ancient Sycamore tree stands sentinel.
It guards the hill for more than 200 years,
On this 100-year-old farm.

She commands the holler from her perch.
Late each day I look out
from the upper window of the farmhouse,

And study her huge limbs.
Outstretched up and down alike.
Sometimes broken. Sometimes bare.
Always stately with the huge white trunk,

And butter light etching the
Leaves most times of year.
The storms have ripped

through time and time again.
Each time she heals herself.
Regains her composure.

Not so other trees.
I've dined beneath the generous
boughs of an oak in summer,

And seen her obliterated into splinters in
a spring storm by the next year.
I know she saw the Civil War.

Watched all the soldiers marching home,
In rags and blood-stained raiment,
Down the country lane, past our farm.

Sometimes I hear the porch swing stir.
As though someone had stopped to rest
Wounded. Fatigued with weary bones.

Despaired of the losses of the men,
And children -of the land.
After all.
After all the cold and starvation and hope and prayers.
My sycamore tree –
200 years of strong.

13

LAWS OF NATURE ARE HARSH

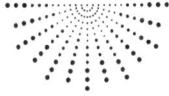

Healers heal.
And God's in charge.
The young calf, fuzzy like a sheep.
Like a lost lamb. Curly, silver grey hair.
He couldn't stand
lost in the field abandoned by his mother,
Hard to hand feed with a plastic bottle.
But once the mama's left
him out alone in the field.
What you gonna do?
Blue Daze we called him then.
Winds howl around the barn door,
And rain began to fall.
I prayed for this rain,
to end the drought.
I tried to explain—
Endless lush fields of green
to this young babe.
His eyes wide and brown.

Who'd been born into the cold brown fields
of winter and loneliness.
Please stay. As the rain fell, soft thudding on the metal roof.
The babe slept. The final sleep.

14

SNOWLESS WINTER'S DAY

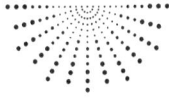

If it were snow out there,
Making sun bounce back to the sky,
all glows white
with shadows purple.
If it would snow,
I would don my parka,
My hat, scarf, and gloves.
I would smile into the stinging snow
As I climb the hill with frozen feet.
Snow shouts come out!
Play snow games,
Like angels.
Don't hide away
In your cold abode,
Fingers gone numb
clutching the pen.
In an effort to pen stark winter words down,
On white lined paper.
Hoping for a snow

or an interruption,
someone to pass by,
a soul who may want a bit of soup,
or a taste of buttery warmth.
Two souls together,
To light the spark.
In the embers of a drenched dreary day
Slipping icy into night.

SOUTHERN WINTER BLUES

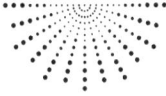

*S*outhern Winter Blues

The grey sky was endless
The bitter cold held on with ice shard blasts
That crept beneath the skin,
Bone brittle ice wind.
Silent thick gray, like snow-blanket clouds.
But no snow fell to warm the frozen dirt and dry bits of dead grass
That covered the frozen fields.
I gazed at lonely black winter branches
scrawling long messages into the white sky.
Yet I found no answers in the stillness.
Wet rain hit the metal roof with icy pings.
We watched each other's faces.
We longed for the soft loveliness
snowfall like feathers
The daffodils buttery heads smiling with a bit of color,
Dotting the wet, mud slicked hill.

A winter that fell directly from summer into cold.
staying tenacious as a bulldog that won't let go.
Only warm enough to melt snow
But no sunshine through the gloom
Southern winter blues.

16
TODAY

Often as I walk the forest
I find my path blocked by a fallen tree.
Each day I give it a wide berth
changing my path and cutting through the woods.
But today I stopped to look

at the wounded tree, the huge scar,
a jagged rip, on the ancient cedar,
With the roots completely gone.
Gnarled branches on the massive trunk
Jab like spikes toward the sky.
The woods fall away for it to rest.

Today
 the snow glistens on its dark age.
The wind moans to the sky.
The forest cradled him like the Pieta.
All the sunlight is orange thru stained glass branches.
The dark shapes in the shadows mourn his loss.

Shadows fall
While leaves have fallen and wind has blown them far
The speechless tree upon the earth lays bare.
The forest floor
Has called him home.

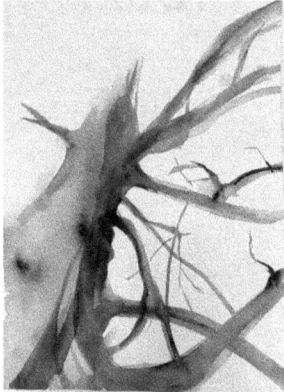

MEDITATION

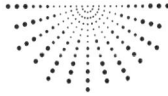

Resting in the forest
On a log seat
I shut my eyes tight.
Poetry flowed. Yet, I,
Pen less
listened to each bird's voice.

Quiet, demanding, whispering, or loud.
I only knew a few
Of their names by heart.

I wondered if there was a sound dictionary,
For knowing birdcalls.
My eyes flew open to watch the woods

Looking for heart shapes in the trees,
Or drawn by tangled vines.
The blackness in the trunk hollow,
My gaze intent,

In case some light
Or creature would suddenly appear
here, in the winter wood.

The forest has spent her gold now.
Leaves of all nations and tribes lay together
In a tangled orgy of pattern.
Brown, crisp and dry underfoot.
Meditation on silence.
So smooth
I could hear the walnut trunk I leaned on
Breathing.
Its branches, a scrawled black message
Against the chill, white, sky.

PART III
NARRATIVE

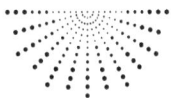

5

THE COWBOY AND THE GYPSY

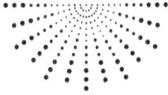

There is a lone star shining in the southwestern sky.
There's a Lone Star café just off Broadway.
Held from one another in a time worn distance.
Held from dreams not yet announced.
She with courage to do it alone.
He with a courage to stay at home.

The cowboy and the Gypsy held their meetings on the moon.

Love me quietly she said hold me gently.
Icy winds and grey streaked streets.
Camp coffee books blankets and furs.
Exhaust fumes taxis and beggars stare.
Clover fed cattle, a new colt, He gazing out at his farm.
She sent him a letter on the wind.
Cooler than the wind, he said
Over water she is.
Music can make you or break you.
Dance with me, she said. So close and hold me.
Tight they were yet so far.

Both of them watching that lone star.

He waited for a sign.
He hoping for more than a memory.
She cried, play me a song I can cry to.
Tears in the river one drop at a time;
South Canadian memories, pounding hooves on sand.
He gave them his soul
they gave him a hand.

The Cowboy and the Gypsy held there meetings on the mews.

Love me gracefully she said, touch me calmly.
Old rustic places in big open spaces.
Thoughts as big as the sky.
The morning sun. A bird at the sill. A message from him
      to you.
Midnight blue feeling an all-encompassing hue.
Midnight cowboys, gypsy's, and blues.

The Cowboy and the Gypsy headed for a place they knew.

There's a lone star shining in the Southwestern sky,
a beckoning light for you, for I
have found a new Horizon.
Purples and mauves gently sunsets curve into distance.
Dance.
With me she said fiercely, fire in her glance.
The Cowboy's calm blue gaze possessed her.
And the dark horse pounds its hooves against the earth.

6

JONATHAN

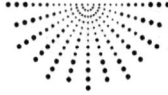

First Grade Uniforms
All untucked
Standing. Watching.
Others play recess.
I back up. So not to be hit
or knocked over.
No one knows I'm there.
I stare.

Desks in rows,
Chalk dust, squeaky letters,
Brown paper crinkles with
peanut butter smells.
Special all School Lunch
for the Christmas holiday.
The crowds of tables
loud with shouts.
Classes follow in lines.
Soon I'm lost.

Staring over at all the chaos
with Christmas trees and cardboard stars.
I lost my line. My class. I see my friend.
My long-lost Jonathan
from kindergarten days.
We sat beside each other
every day back then.

He cracks a grin
when his eyes spot mine
behind his dark brown bangs.
His shirt white and buttoned crooked.
We find no one cares. If we eat together now.
I see his dark hair, his white skin
with scuffed up knees.
Like mine.
My food can hardly fit in my mouth
I'm smiling so big.
The rest of the world swam round and round
behind him and me like the periphery.
He filled my vision and my heart.
Time seemed to stop.
All I knew was him.

Trudging back and forth
to school and home for days.
Dreary homework. Tedious thoughts,
with hands raised till your arm aches.
All fell away and disappeared
on that miraculous day.

Each day thereafter
I searched the lines.
Hoping I would find my friend.
Once I spotted him far off.
Someone was pushing him

in his wheelchair. I didn't know.
I waited and wondered.

Then one day he was gone.
Forever.
So young.
Only six years old. So brave.
Multiple Sclerosis, someone said.

7

MOSS

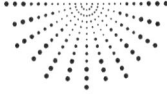

The angel stood, head bowed,
Over the stones in the garden.
Lifelike in the curve of his head,

The arch of the wings,
Folded almost in prayer.
Still yet stone.

I looked at the stones on the ground,
Etched and marked with names obscured
with time and moss.
"Gravestones." Kat said.

I jumped off the path.
Sorry to trespass upon a sacred place.
"I buried six here.

"I brought them from New Jersey
When I moved to Tennessee."
Six cats.

"Brought all my koi fish too.
Twenty-four in a tank. They made the long journey
in a rented van.

"I had three cats in a cooler.
Dead cats. On ice." She explained.
Mysterious motivations?
or Egyptian in her past life?

8

OPHELIA LIVES AGAIN

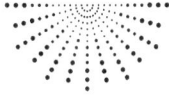

Seven royal folk standing on a raft
Dressed in purple, red, emerald, and royal blue
floated silently upon green water
In the dim evening light.
Trunks thick with green.
Mossy limbs extend abundant arms
Overhead and down into the water.

The river calm as glass.
But no glass ever looked so green.
Framed in gnarled root legs
poking knees above the surface.
Laughing folk, slender, and elegant,
Stick pole push-pushing them along
as they glide across still water.

Eyes hidden in thick brush watch.
Grey sky is lost from view
Somber sun already sunk
Beyond the distant edge.

Evening brings a calm upon the group.

Slender tapered arms bearing jewels.
Casually barefoot women.
The men, sleeves rolled up,
Forearms exposed, Rolex dangling
They clutch each other's hands,
Staring at water.
They dare not fathom what lies beneath.

Suddenly she slipped in at a shallow spot.
Ophelia floated by. All algae and moss
Clinging to her silks,
Laughing she swam about to clean herself up.
She emerged and sat again atop the raft
Her prettily pointed toe,
tipping the water,
While her green tinged blonde hair clung about her.
The laughing party wined and dined
Continuing, on champagne and roses.
At the front of the vessel,
She parted the watery muck with her toe.
And wondered at the world that lie below.
He with serious eyes watched her as all was still.
The vine, and the moss, and the clinging sticks in her hair.

Her cornstarch white arms smudged
With the black-green stuff like bruises
She turned her peach mouth up
Into a smile that shone
And green eyes that glittered
more than any jewel or gold
He could have bought her.

9
THE VISITOR

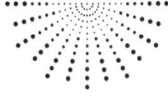

The family of three,
cozy over a November supper.
The wind whistled. There was a knock at the door.

Pleasant exchanges of greetings
echoed from the foyer,
when the mom answered the knock.

The child ate big bites of chicken.
The father's simple meal half consumed,
'Who is it?' he called. reluctant

to arise from the table.
It's Tommy. He looks well.
Better dressed than before,

with a coat and shoes on.
Tommy is the only one who comes to the door,
explanations ensue. We give him a few dollars
and he's on his way.

We offered him jobs in the summer.
Mowing the lawn. Gardening.
He says no.
On the subway in New York

A black man was begging (for his food),
from the passengers.
One man stood up and said,
Get a job!

The man glanced down at his brother's shiny patent leather
    loafers.
I'm on my way to work.
I earned these shoes I'm walkin' in.
I won't give you a dollar.
No sir!

THE SOUL OF ATLANTA

"The Soul of Atlanta burned
During the Civil War,"
Dawn said.
She said it like a mantra
Thinking of Buckhead
wrapped in freeways and knotted with cars
And the traffic moving at the speed of feet per hour.
How do you find the soul of a town
wrapped in exhaust fumes
and designer faux firs?

Atlanta is gone with the wind
and burned in the flame
of Scarlett's burning desire.
In search of the old and the deep
South of our hearts
We can go to Savannah.

Savannah with her heavily treed squares
Her boughs weighted with moss

Celtic songs and penny whistles
Playing by the fountain running gold
With 100-year-old water.
Cobblestone streets and open carriages
Pulled by heavy grey drafts.
Mansions intact three stories tall.
Boxwood, gardenia, and wisteria trellis
frame lawns of cheek-soft grass.

11

CHRYSTAL BRIGHT

THEY MET AT THE FUNERAL,
her heels were high,
the path to the grave site rocky.
As she was the preacher,
and he was the son. It was his duty
to throw her on his steed
and carry her gallantly to the podium.
Where she would speak
encouraging words to the living
about the life of the dead.

He had no steed.
But he held out his arm
and escorted her gallantly
as he could with a slight limp,
up to the front of the crowd,
to the top of the hill.
So she could look down
upon the family gathered to hear
words of praise about their Pa.

After such auspicious beginnings
it was quite natural
that they should date.
Tentative meetings for coffee
With her heavy teaching-- preaching schedule.
At first. With a name like Chrystal
She was perfect for him. He saw the light.
Light to transform his once dark hope
into bright futures. And miracles to come.
As they said "I do."

12
WINDOWS OF THE PAST

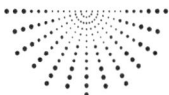

TRAVELING IN TRAINS
inspire me to stare.
Out of the window.as the train moves on.
I put my book down.
The rhythmic click upon the tracks
are a metronome to memory.

Yet the landscapes out the window
of Italian trees and Tuscan hills
are so foreign to my normal
site and sounds, I think
I am staring out at the past.
At the world of Michelangelo

and Saint Francis of Assisi.
I can see them just beyond
the red roofed stucco town.
Somewhere they're healing the sick
or preparing an impasto
to adorn some forgotten Popes ceiling.

The Tuscan poplar trees, manicured and perfect
like spires lining simple roads
that lead to vineyards. And donkeys
carrying sticks the old widow in black
still uses
to light her fires in the night.

I find it strange.
That what you think about,
like Michelangelo. Seems still alive.
Ever present in your heart.
Like when I paint the figure
to paint and draw like him

Is what I strive for.
I wonder about his life;
His work; his pain.
The years upon his back with that ceiling
I never got to see. Because they
were picking the Pope that day

In St. Peters square.
The oval to embrace the crowds.
'Fuma Bianca,' someone called,
'Fuma Bianca.'
The crowd went wild.

13

MOTHER'S HEART

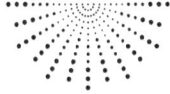

A babe was born in a cave
lying in a manger
long ago. As everyone seems to know.
I heard tell of another child
born in a cave in Poland in 1942.
The parallel is they both were Jews.
Funny how that worked.
Both babes born
to loving mothers' centuries apart.

Persecution by Romans or Nazis
the oppressor still roams the earth.
The latest ruler of the day,
to claim his power demand we pay.
It was the Roman Catholic Christians
who helped the babe that day.
The Egyptian princess saved Moses
in the reeds.
The wise men brought gifts for a king.

Fathers, Mothers,
Sons, and daughters,
Thirty people or more,
Stayed safe throughout the war.
Three years of days into nights
all dark
Perhaps the crack of light
meant rescue, food, or exposure.

Each day after day
the Earth held her children close.
Earth as mother of the lost and found.
Generations of families held within.

All survived to tell the tale.
Moses, Jesus, or John Claude,
Angel of darkness rules his legions in the world.
Whereas enlightened truth is found within.
Each precious heart beating life
within each tiny breast.
Each the spark,
The light of joy
within their mothers' heart.

14

THE MINE SHAFT OF MY DREAMS

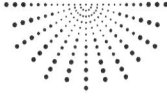

As I meditate in silence,
I am aware of sound.

Tambourine jingle of the red leaves,
the wind chime carried by the breeze.
The purple pansy touches petals
in a silent clap.
Far from here
in the cave at the edge of the woods,
twenty feet down and tucked inside
all is still, and must, and dark.

The time you looked at me with pain,
And wonder held your stare.

Not one word was said.
How my heart filled my throat,
as doubt and hope
clamored for meaning
in that ominous quiet.

I found silence once,
deep below the earth. Having traveled
through mine shafts and tunnels.
There, surrounded by darkness
of the deep dream,
A lone diamond shone.
Crystalline light glistened
from within.

Meditating on silence,
I could hear.

I listened to the voice of the spring
slipping a steady rhythm
through white rocks into clear pools.
Caught in the tangle of sound
the wind chimes join in,
flowing with pure water
to the hidden place that swallows sound.

The leaves rise to a crescendo,
dancing with the wind off the ground.
The strange bleating goat
hollers through the holler.
The finch on the bare limb
calls a song to me.

And then I remembered.
The stare.
Your eyes. Wounded. Longing
in awe and disbelief, wonder, hope
and deep desire.
All was silence.
As my heart stopped still.

15

OUTSIDE DINING

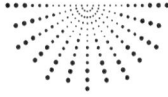

Eating outside on the New Orleans balcony
Overlooking the square,
Amused by the bee
intrigued by my dish.

Steak sizzled black and blue
arranged on garlic mashed potatoes.
Wood worn and thick,

A narrow balcony angled down with years.
Carved newel posts held us on.
Tall walls of bricks stood firm
200 years or more.

Autumn-yellow leaves, cobalt sky,
Crisp breeze, and the bee were here today.
Caught in the trance of the moment,

On an edifice that knew 1000 days.
Solid treads of stairs stepped

All the way to the top.

Holding her stories in the curve of the wood.
Thank God man doesn't need
To renovate everything

All the time. I do not think
the moment would taste as wonderful
Presented any other way.

16

WATER DANCE

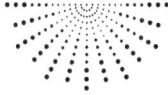

Following the call of the drum
thru the town
we found the spring

Beside which the town was founded.
Rock cliffs recalling Indian days
surround a pool

of goldfish flown in from Japan.
It's the kind of world we live in.
Past visions of Indians gathered round

the spring to bathe or drink
before the settlers came.
Tall brick city walls now crowd around her.

Yet sitting by silvery spring water
I face rock cliff ledges holding sunlight.
Her creviced face bares offerings

of sage grass and moon flowers.
We watch the mallard flaunt his wings
While ducks dance and bob around him.

Couples, kids, and teens gather for an evening stroll.
The drum circle grows larger.
Triangle and symbol make the beat sound like Brazil.
After all it's an urban city center,
Past and present tied together.

17

WISE CIRCLE OF FRIENDS

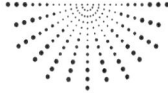

They will never accept you
in your own hometown.
It's the sign of the times.

No one ever gave Him
a place at the Inn.
To be shunned or ignored

is standard fare for prophets.
At a time when the truth
is too hard to hear.

Only the very brave hearts
Seek wisdom
Won't run or hide

As they listen to your talk
With minds open wide.

THE DWELLING PLACE

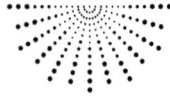

Leaves are billowing thru
The abandoned shell
Of empty warehouse lying bare.

Barren rooms of neglect.
Dried. Brown and rusty crunch of leaves
Room after room beyond room.

High ceilinged lofty space
Crusty with neglect.
The nest now empty.

The bird has flown.
In the stillness of debris
I find a place,

Large, open, window filled and dusty.
I long to clean the soiled glass.
To scrub.

To sweep the corners
of this foreign empty place.
I wonder why this art studio lies bare.

No longer smells of oils and turpentine
Colored blues, purples, and reds
squeezed out upon the palette.

Where has the Muse gone?
That once sat, legs crossed,
with dusky laugh upon the edge?

The dank smell reminds me
of ghosts that scared the joy away.
Music shall be played

upon the black and white keys
Gleaming in the grand piano.
Convening in the light-filled Southern room.

Music to fill the cavernous mansion vibrates.
Echoing out to the barren life
That dwells far but near

in that parallel universe of memory.
Music brings the muse
To fill the space and light the souls

Reclaim the dwelling place once more.

19

MAN WITH THE ARK IN ALABAMA

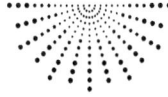

There is a stranger at the reading
from Athens, Alabama.
He came amongst us with a tale.

He lives upon an ark, he says,
he built with his own hands
placed snug within the hill.

Windows open wide to the southern sun
to warm the family of ten who dwell within.
His wife bore him seven sons

and a daughter for her comfort.
He is proud of all their skills
and who they have become.
Although his blonde-white hair hangs long,

and his wisdom blue eyes pierce
through a mop of beard.
It gives you some idea of all the years

the weathered cheeks have kept good cheer.
He tells of horses, cows, chickens
and the water buffalo, he keeps watered

with long hauls from stream to field.
He plows to keep his family fed
on their backwoods Alabama holding.

The hand-built home is big and long,
enough to house them all now grown.
I want to see this rustic place,

surrounded by barns and powered by solar.
Everything designed for off-grid living.
Prepared to brave all kinds of storms,

Political or weather.

20

UNINVITED GUEST

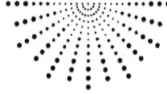

The Poet as a guest
Whose tongue unloosed with wine

Outpours his heart
For all to hear.

And when it's time to wind down.
You can't get a word in anyway

He wants more
- to say
- to drink.

So you place another log on the fire.
In doing so, feed the flame.

Watch as eyes grow wide, with nameless desire.
And though you don't believe a word of it
you write it all down.

Till its early morning
and you want to hide your head
while it's still dark.

You find a blanket and sleep
cuddled up on the couch.
Like a babe whose soul can rest.

FULL OF PROMISE

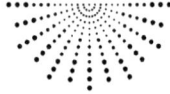

The guests have left.
The children all packed up.
Tucked into cars

with cries and toys buckled in with them.
The day looms long
full of promise and thoughts unsaid.

Space in the day created
for new bird song.
Wind blows old leaves

A rustle and a whisper.
A strand of hair blows across my face.
That crow barks like a dog.

A trucks distant whine is long gone.
Trees jangle leaves like a thousand tambourines.
as the sun in the blue sky hides her face

Like a shy girl behind her veil.
Are all the fairies dancing in the branches
excited for my attention?
Now that friends have gone.

22

THE SERMON

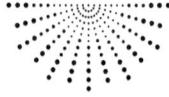

In Sewanee
The Church of The Apostles
sends wood gables arching towards the sun.

All was silent. Expectant like a breath caught and held.
Two cars full of cousins and family
ambled in from the crisp fall air.

Silly talk slowed to a stop
as blue jean clad sullen teenagers
take a break from their I-pods.

Polished flagstone floors in autumn hue
Like a forest floor.
Tapered slender wood trusses span the width.

Columns march towards an alter
filled with silent choir benches.
The ever-reaching gables

frame the view of a forest gone golden.
Beyond the suspended wood
of the cross.
Where although resurrected,

Jesus reminds us of the path.
A voice echoed in the subdued hush
Loud and clear
The man at the podium began to speak

address the empty room
and all of nature thru the glass.
Everyone found a seat and sat entranced,

letting the impromptu sermon tell the story
of the world gone wrong.
Ages upon ages, Saint upon saints,

Man can still be saved
with the simple path
of the carpenter's son.

23

THE COMMUNITY OF THE ESSENNES

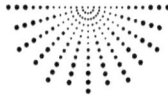

Jars full of wine,
Trees full of olives,
Oils for anointing the chosen one.
Oil lamps with crystal flame,
Ages upon ages,
Prophets foretelling prophets.

One man's destiny,
To save the world.
In time. The fire of passions revealed.
Find the truth in a burning bush.
The stories on scrolls,
Writings in Hebrew, Aramaic and Greek.

Secrets held in jars buried deep
Hidden in caves.
The hidden knowledge is within,
Someone said.
Mary immaculate. Baby born bearing light.
We look to the heavens to find the star.

One star foretold by the seers.
Our sun is a star.
God's Son the illuminated One.

Jars full of stories
Flowing from lips
Like wine flows from rivers of time.
Water into wine. The grape - the vine.
The truth foretold long ago by prophets.
One man is Divine. The purity of the line,

From the house of David.
Generations of tales, parables and truths,
Spring fountains of pure water,
Held in the center of the desert town.
Grapes and olives and wheat are grown like a prayer.
Women and men as equals

Debate in long conversations
In the central square.
All understand the cosmos.

With telescopes and models to study the stars.
The earth and ten planets orbit the sun.
How did they know that way back then?
The Essenes message of peace
Is yet to be revealed.
Or understood.

24

BOY KING

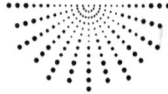

Our boy king turned president
Trumped the polls,
With sleight of hand tricks
And treats while the people live

A nightmare carnival
From Halloween to Mardi-gras.
Tricksters get a free lunch.
Entitled millennials love the

Disaster politics that can disrupt
The status quo. Indicted school Marm
Candidate with her lists and agendas
Must take a back seat.

While no one gets a free lunch.
The aliens still land in Peru
Infiltrating South America.
The Russians make peace pacts

And the cold war and the new deal
Turn to ash in the face of the neo
Nazi socialist cosmology.
Monsanto can now feed the world

Thanks to GMO.
And the illegal aliens die
On the other side of the new wall.

25

DEERFIELD MORNING

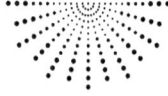

Eyes opened fast to great the day.
The sun shone through hemlock arms
Of the tree outside my window.

Whip, slap, creak went the branch against the pane.
The sound called me to wakefulness.
First disoriented, I stared

At the abstract shapes of black branches and stained-glass-
      window light.
Then my feet hit the cold bare floor.

I tiptoed out.
So not to wake
Gabrielle who slept in the top bunk

With Anna curled like a ball
In her toddlers bed.
The floors creaked. I went

Out to the dining room.
I pressed my face against the glass
Wet on my nose
As I saw the first purple plums

Hanging heavy on the tree.
An endless day of possibility
Opened before me.

I wondered if Rita
would want to play today?
I had my sand box city all laid out.

With houses stacked on top like boxes.
More like the adobe dwellings of the pueblo in New Mexico.
The Old Indian Chief there

Had praised my black hair
And fresh white skin. He placed a red beaded
Medallion necklace upon my chest.

His thick black braids were like ropes.
And tons of feathers on his crown.

The city project was large.
With roads Gabrielle and I
drove our toy cars through.

I dreamed of cities in the snow
I would make
When winter came again.

The smells of coffee perking filled the air
and I knew my Father was awake.
A moment longer I would wait.

Enjoy the silent house
a moment more.

PIANO HANDS

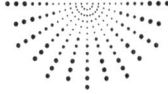

My Father could dance like Zorba,
His hands up clapping, shaking his head with that full beard,
His hips marking the music.
My Mother on the other hand…
Her fingers made love to the piano.
Keys, black and white floating effortlessly
into music in the air.
Nights when all nine of us were tucked in bed,
She played.

Hands that dressed us, fed us, and sent us off
to school. To play, to be.
Big warm, soft and long fingered,
white with the purity of prayer.
She knelt down each night,
her rosary beads draped like Spanish moss,
eyes closed. The silver cross swung heavy.
I prayed daily for a handsome prince

with chivalry and graceful bearing,

to rescue us from the life we shared.

Money flowed back and forth like waves
Never filling the coffers
of sand holes dug deep.
But making it all disappear.

We laughed and danced by the sea.
Every Sunday. So much fun for free.
Nature was our playground and our guardian.
When you empty your heart to the sea,
it flows back and fills you with strange
melody.
Or secret longings you should never speak.

And so we dug into our lives. All week,
Seven sisters, joined by the ones in the sky at night.
Seven daughters all filled with dance and art
and poetry.
Cleaning, washing, cooking, gardening,
diapers, feedings, games and song.
All week long.
The Sunday stationwagon filled with joy,
Watermelons, hotdogs, and chips,
backpacks, beach blankets, and toys.
Sandcastles, swimming, and walks by the sea.

Live with gusto, work with passion,
play with bliss.
That is how a single Mom with nine kids,
goes with the flow.
With the patience of the waves,
back and forth and out to sea.
All in constant motion. Don't miss a beat,
when you play that song.

SHE WROTE NOTHING

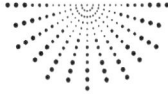

FOR THE SAKE OF THE POEM,
I wrote my Mother was a poet.
But in truth,
My Mother was a philosopher.
And in so being lived her life.
She married her man,
gave birth to nine children.
She taught school, and played piano
at night while we all drifted off to sleep
in our cozy cocoons.

In such a life of teaching
And speaking and rearing
And living,
She wrote nothing down.

As I turned toward adulthood
and entered fresh into that world,
I always felt wise beyond my years.
Full of her healer gypsy-grandmother's remedies.

I sang her favorite folk songs by Joan Baez and Peter Paul and
    Mary.
I'd heard Plato and Aristotle quoted and paraded
before me any time we argued, or debated.
She reared us with the wisdom
of the prophet from Kahlil Gibran.

We discussed and disputed as we prepared evening meals
and tucked the little ones into their beds.
Bedtimes of hot baths —rub-a-dub-dub 4 kids in a tub.
Warm milk and honey to sweeten their dreams,
Breakfasts of oatmeal with cinnamon and raisins,
Café au lait in my thermos for lunch.
For the sake of the poem I said my mom was a poet.
In truth she is a philosopher
And the tome she wrote was me.

RITA OF THE BACKYARD SCRAMBLE

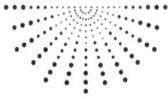

Rita of the backyard scramble
The neighborhood queen.
Hair black and shiny short
Like the tomboy she was.
We traveled far behind the houses
In all the connecting backyards.

We raced down the street
Collecting children from our block.
If we had ten we had enough for two teams.
Crab-apple war,
Or rover, red rover let Johnny come over.
The fear of the capture

Grateful to be called back.
She kept her eye on me.
I was always on her team.
She fast and thin and three years older
Somehow let me join in

despite my white skin
To her Italian tan.

Rita was the best friend
I could never replace.
Once we moved down south,
left Deerfield for good.
Her house was full of boys,
Carpet, and a color TV.

Her mom made white bread sandwiches
that stuck to your teeth.
Rita never stayed inside.
The street was our world.
Brave together we went far.
Once we stood outside the witch's house.

Our bellies itched as we lay in the grass
Behind the hedge in an abandoned field,
Watching the leaded windows of mystery.
The house of stone with a steep pointy roof.
A thick oak front door.
The witch emerged in a flowered kimono

Grabbed up all her mail
and melted back inside.
Witch? thought I
In deep disappointment.
Wondering if loneliness and widowhood
made everyone so.

LONG WALK HOME

*L*ONG WALK HOME

On being eight
on the long walk home,

Beside the bayou, my satchel bumping
my mosquito bitten legs.

The walk made longer
by the drab nothingness.

The sameness of the houses on repeat.
Jorn's street.

Houses stamped from the same mold.
In the same brick.

Endlessly repeating themselves.
Along the wide flat street of new concrete.

Nothing but coarse grass and new trees.
New school smelling of wet asphalt,
And fresh paint.

My thermos full
Of hot coffee-milk gone tepid.

30

PACKING UP MOM'S STUFF

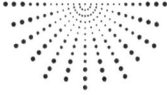

In the old glory hole in the attic
We got lost in the summer heat.
In the house with you gone now so sudden.
And we giggling sisters sticking it through
Hour after hour and mounds of stuff.
The treasures in the attic
Anna and I found after the others
Had left for the day.
The letters gave us your past.
The life before us.
The love letters from Frankie in college
In Notre Dame
He called you Kriz. Who's he? who's she?
And ones from your own mother.
Penned in her beautiful hand
On stationary from big hotels from Chicago to New York.
Your life so full of us
You seldom ventured down the road of memory
And we only knew you as Mother.

Some of the letters took hold and grabbed my soul
          Clenched it like a vice
A history I had never known.
Our brother Raphael,
Sent away young. Only fourteen.
As a single mom
Perhaps you were at a loss with a boy
In a world of sisters.
Must have never learned to spell.
A shame for the son of an English teacher.
I read the first note confused.
Deer Mom, Gabrielle and Tom are fine.
The weather is cool here for Texas,
The garden is growing fine,
I miss you. When can I come home?
I struggled thru letter after letter.
Anna, I said did you know Raph was gone in 1977?
I read more. Soon I saw a multitude.
Piles of small white envelopes
Each with a square of white paper.
I removed and unfolded each in turn.
Letter after letter after letter.
Small like the doves you find inside a sand dollar.
Soon like snowflakes
The multitude of white speckled the upstairs room.
I miss you. When can I come home?
I know for a fact he never came home.
Until he was 16
Even then he got a job nearby
At an Arabian horse farm.
He lived in a trailer and cooked his meals on a hotplate.
He traveled the fields
And hiked the woods.

He had no car, no parent.
He taught himself the world.
Thru nature, plants and wild deer
He met along the way.
I miss you. When can I come home?
What part of him died back then?
Things I never knew until you died today.

31

LOSS

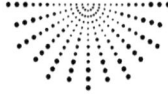

Left like water filling sand holes
By the shore.
Erasing every trace
Of the hole I spent all day
Filled with hope
In the stinging sun
Digging.

MESSAGES IN TREES FOR NICOLE

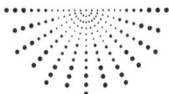

Black tree branches held the white night.
Sky caught in a tangle.
The tangled lace of trees
Against the cottony cloud filled night.

I thought of balmy summer evenings
Spent outside on the porch nursing
The patient peace of full night air.
The supper done.

The lettuce growing in rows,
With mosquitoes held at bay by yellow candles,
The night moon lost on its way up.
One more song.

No one cares if we stay out a little long,
Before bath time and bed.
We celebrate.
One night in early summer holds the promise

Of endless nights and timeless ends.

Your father will go back to the studio,
And I will put you two to bed.
But now, the space between the crickets
And the notes on the guitar is full.

Fullness being a magnetic something
That makes the nothing that surrounds us
Hold our breaths.

33

FLASH

My daughter is a photographer
because my dad was a photographer.

My son is a filmmaker
because my mother was a poet.

Black-and-white
Stark and bright
the story of our lives
is in the image.

Dark night surrounds a silver sliver moon
 like shards of wisdom
pierce hearts caught
in the flash of illuminating youth.

THE GUEST

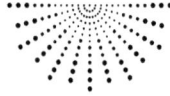

I love the guest.
The idea of a visitor
Coming into the yellow light
from the cold.
Night after night,
Dinners of fragrant soups
and healthy breads.
Give us, oh Lord, our daily bread.
Thank you for the farm we live on.

We have killed the fatted calf.
The prodigal son has returned abundant.
Our coffers runneth over,
The store house is full, with jars of time.
Fertile valleys and springs full of promise.
Coddled by gilded trees filled with light.

Life sits on the edge of the tongue.
Like a thought barely formed, heart-felt
Yet feels like destiny.

A heart full of anticipation
of the knock at the door.
To welcome the guest into our midst.
To share our daily bread.
And dine at our table.

SPRING GRAVE; IN MEMORIAM

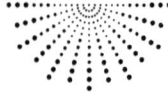

Waiting by the graveside
at the cemetery of my kinfolk.
Lost in thought of the memory

Of great grandparents and aunts and cousins long gone.
Some of whom I only knew by story.
I stare out at the spring grass

Encircling tombstones.
Names and angels etched in stone
Gleaming in the rain that whispered

lightly from sky to earth.
Then a car went round my truck.
It jerked my mind back to the present.

I had stopped my work
On an ordinary day,
The trailer behind me loaded with fresh wood.

I had stepped from routine to stop by.
And say hay.
Greet those who had traveled these roads,

And worked and prayed in these hills
in times gone by.
As time goes by.

36

SORROW

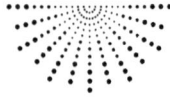

*S*ORROW

My sorrow when she's here with me
  Is a happy time. I court her coming.
  Brewing Earl grey tea
  With just a hint of honey.

  My straight back chair pressed
  Close to the cold glass,
  Where prism raindrops fall and run
  Streaming down with grace.

  Taking me to the place of screaming
  At the loss of what he took from me.
  I am frozen, numb to that abuse.

  The warm hues and red and blue
  of a Pissarro winter Landscape

Touch my heart deep.
As if I were beside him
Painting twentieth century Paris.

What he tried to take,
I stepped aside and let it go.
My conviction solid, sure.
About what should be mine.

If it's truly mine it can't be taken.
I watch the parallel in other people's stories.

Italian Villa awaits.
Or perhaps a summer on the Amalfi coast.
A place where I can bring my brushes,
My oils, my canvas, and my heart.

My muse will travel too.
Like a secret hidden in a sacred place.
Knowing that you know.
The beauty in the making
The beauty of the living it.

My mind traces the far black branch
Of the distant maple.
There on the edge is the robin.
Her breast a ruby red in the grey sky.

Like the blood I must shed.
Upon each creation
For it to live.

37

CLUTTER

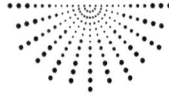

The clutter of my life
Makes me run away.

Running Away is my go-to.
It's the horse-fear predator–prey story.

Flight or Freeze.
Of the lost deer.

Bravado and acting as-if
Has kept smiles plastered

To a face like a mask.
Of "Me too'. 'Not me.'

I longed to be an actress
But wasn't up for the casting couch.

It's a known fact.

To play the game you must be a player.

'Not me,'
And I stepped to the sidelines.

Not an actress
Not even a corporate ladder climber.

A married girl
Hiding in the hills.

With pen in hand, I cling to each
Bit of memory and pages of story,

Stacks of short stories, novellas, and poems.
All a pile- written and edited, read and reread.

The pile of paintings filling my rooms
Makes me afraid to go home.

So, I hide in crowded café's
And chilly Starbucks,

Writing new dreams
Dreaming new stories
While frozen in place
Like a deer.

Or running from life like a horse.
I'm afraid to go home.

You say 'me too', I say 'not me',
As I step out of life.

UNION STATION

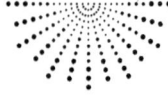

On a smoky cloudy day I drove
Into the cold
To east Nashville.
I passed Union Station.
The tall spire has been standing
Piercing the grey skies of dusk.
Since 1900,

Bringing passengers in
From Cincinnati or Chicago.
The blare of the train whistle and the crowds
Covered the patterned tile floor
With clattering feet and black winter coats.

Men smoked cigars on the balcony above
And checked their pocket watches
To be sure it was all on time.
A huge fireplace built by the town's best masons
Boasted a fiery blaze.

The Childs fist clutched in the warm big hand
Of his father as he trotted too fast on chubby legs.
The old lank Harry pushed a broom
And winked at the large grey-eyed boy.

The chime and the whistle and the
Red lipsticked woman's perfumed kiss
Still shone crooked on his forehead.
He dropped the coin he was clutching
For the promised ice cream

And a granny with a grey bun
Watched it land heads up.
Here you are she smiled as she tucked it
Safely into his pocket.
His grey eyes connected

With her deep brown ones in the wise face and he didn't cry.
Later he saw those eyes again
In a much younger tanned face.
A vibrant girl with a saucy manner.
He knew better.
He remembered those eyes.
He knew the girl.

LILLIAN ROSE

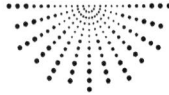

Out of the dark winter
comes a bright light.
Lillian Francis Rose was born
this day joining our family
at this Christmas season.
She embodies the grace
that surrounds our clan.

David's heartfelt struggle
to build a strong sure home.
Blessed by two beautiful babes.
Arthur's cheeks aglow with health.
Eyes intense, dark blue with purpose.
He makes his big bold marks
while we await the birth. His colored drawings
adorn every wall and fill the house.

Lillian appears in Carianne's arms.
Bright and alert she searches the crowd.
Faces of her new family,

she will come to learn
Her mom, dad, and little brother,
grandparents, and aunts,
Kaitlyn and Nicole. Joy spills over
a kind the birthing room can't contain.

A falling star.
The angel has come.
She yearns to give
As well as share
in all of our lives.
In her light, small, tiny-baby-self
Her calm exudes a healing balm
In all those here.

Joyful smiles infect each face
As I glance about the room.
Out of the dark of winter
Comes a bright light
Each new birth a spark
Of the divine.
Babe at Christmas,
She is our present.

40
THE SHORE

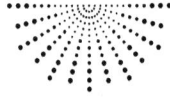

*As I walk along the shore
thinking of my life before
My eyes watch sea-foam
etch the edge of sunlight*

*as it travels back and forth
like liquid silver. Moving light
Mesmerized upon
the water of magnetic motion.*

*B*Y THE SEASHORE A STORM BREWS

41

THE STORY OF DIEGO JACKSON

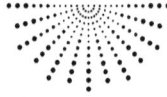

*D*iego Jackson hailed from a small southern town in Tennessee. His mother was a Spanish beauty and his devoted Dad a farmer, slaving for the kids to have shoes and a solid education. Diego was presently living in Murfreesboro, the seat of Middle Tennessee State University. He had completed his education and held a fine degree. In fact, he was the first in his family to hold a university degree. He knew stuff, too much stuff. He had sailed through as a star student.

He lived in this wonderful old yellow house in an historic neighborhood downtown. He'd managed to snag a room up on the third floor during his last semester. Now he looked forward to a year of full-time painting. He was an artist bound for graduate school, a master's degree, and a painting career.

He avoided home. His mother's beautiful face looked so sad. She was always made-up and dressed for perfection whenever his parents visited. It seemed he was somehow a kind of disappointment. The last time he'd seen his dad it shocked him as he saw the aging that stress and the high costs of living had taken. His hair was more salt than pepper these last few years.

Diego had saved his few dollars, spending wisely. He eked out a living by doing contract painting work. It was hard work. Often standing on ladders in scorching summer heat. Paint fumes clogging his brain. He saw visions. He couldn't explain it. He had to paint. Now that it would soon be fall and winter would follow, he planned to hole up in here undisturbed and make it work. Part of him wondered if half of his dad's stress wasn't caused by the effort of putting a smile on that beautiful oval of his mother's face. He wasn't planning to marry or embark on that road of compromise. His life was one of sole dedication and purpose.

He concentrated on the work at hand. He had the whole third floor of the house to himself. He had a small kitchen, a sink and a hot plate in one dormer area. And he had a small single mattress on the floor of another alcove. The main expense had been installing the huge north skylight on the roof. The old attic was all sturdy wood beams. The wide plank wood floors were oak, polished with time. He covered the floors with drop cloths. He covered all the walls and sloping ceiling with drop cloths.

And then he began to paint. He painted long hours. He stretched canvases and filled them with images. His paintings got larger and larger. His arms swept over the canvas in huge sweeps of pure joy. Trees, plants, and hills, animals, suns and moons appeared under his brush. He painted until he couldn't see strait. Then he would rest. He'd sleep and dream. In the mornings ravenous he would make strong coffee and study the paintings in the morning light. While he ate a healthy breakfast. His Mom and Dad had taught him that much.

He was leaning out of the window by his kitchen, trying to get some air to flow in as a break from the late September heat. He spotted a figure in the distance walking down the street. He straightened and watched as the figure, no it was two figures, approached. There was something compelling in the way the woman walked.

He could see her dark hair flying as she hurried down the street with a big woosh of energy. He had stopped mid-stroke in his panting. He was struck. This big ball of energy moving down the street was captivating. Ah, the young one with her was just a child on a bike or a toy car. It was a red bike. He was a young boy, maybe two? Blonde and all boy he could see from here. They were under his window now. He stared down at the pair. He was a bit of a voyeur at times. The bike went by fast. The woman, her white top loose and flying around her as she chased. She grabbed the boy up as they reached the corner. It was the only way to keep the boy from flying across the street unattended. Whoosh. She grabbed him in her arms as a pick-up truck labored past. She held the boy close and hugged him as she spoke. Diego couldn't see her face from here. He was staring in earnest. His dark brew strong and black in his cup. His head tilted forward as he pressed his forehead against the glass pane.

Suddenly, the woman turned and pointed right at the house. She was talking and pointing to the boy. Diego couldn't hear. He jerked back into the shadows nearly spilling his coffee. He caught himself. Surely they couldn't see in. Not when it is bright outside and dark in his attic. He laughed out loud. Turned the radio up and went back to his canvas with bold exuberance. He began to paint.

Diego had created a solid safe room as his studio. He had covered the entire attic floor with drop cloths. He had stapled more drop cloths on the walls. He had then stretched large canvases. There were three 4'x 6', And one 5'x 7'. These he hung from large nails he had pounded into the hard wood. He had clip lights purchased from the hardware store on the square. They clipped to the rafters and beams spanning the attic space. He could angle them as needed to light the surface of his work. This afternoon he had three going at once. He had developed his own technique. With this fall to paint undeterred his style was morphing into a bold expressionism.

He had taken a road trip across the country to visit Graduate schools. He had been from Tennessee to Oklahoma to Mississippi to Louisiana, Houston and Arizona on his travels. The shapes and forms now haunted the landscapes of his paintings. There were the urban city towers of crowded downtowns. The tangle of freeways called the spaghetti bowl, like he had never seen in his Tennessee home town.

There were refineries and smoke stacks, and the Gulf of

Mexico. He had been down there during a spring storm. He'd witnessed the force of waves thrust against the shore amidst rain storms and lightning like fire in the sky. Today as he pulled away from the window, the woman and child now long gone, he could just remember her twisting dancing form as she had sped off into the distance.

He playfully jostled one of the towers in his urban landscape that was taking shape on his canvas.

Fall worked its magic of gold and yellows in the old neighborhood. Diego was hard at work in his treetop studio . Every now and again he caught a fleeting glimpse of the woman and the young boy. But always at a distance. Then fall exhausted itself as the last sugar sweet old maple leaf fell. A bitter winter stole ice fingers on every tree. As his perch was in the treetops he took the cold to heart. Suddenly, in mid-December the bitter cold reality of attics in old houses took hold. There was scant insulation in the rambling ancient yellow house.

He lay shivering in his small bed shoved in a corner. He was only able to paint after work or between jobs. As he was a painter, now that it was winter, he was between jobs. Between jobs and money it seemed. He was one to spend it when he had it, and now he didn't have it. So he wasn't spending, or eating much. He was in the midst of breakthrough paintings. He had seven turned against the walls with four well under way. He even had some new starts. He was struggling with. He was bursting with new images that were a part of his unique process. He wore fingerless gloves in effort to warm his hands. His fingers shook as they held his fat brushes. He took to wearing three shirts, two pair of socks and a sock cap inside. He had a kerosene heater burning constantly. His black canvas hightops were wearing thin.

He stared blankly out of the window at the bare tree tops. He waited and he watched for a sign of the woman and the boy. It's like that sign of life outside kept him company and gave him a sort of hope at the same time. But he never saw the pair through the whole bleak winter. The snow came and blanketed the world. He was snowed in, that suited him. The world from his attic view seemed to be a study in black and white. He painted with a burning focus.

He ate food out of cans. Tuna, Herring fish steaks, raman noodles heated on his hot plate. He didn't really want to go home for Christmas. There was a strange comfort in his loneliness, in his poverty and aloneness. A kind of solace.

His canvas's in turn lost their color. Now he was in a frenzy of smoke stacks and refineries. The red flame peeking from the white on grey on silver – a charcoal world almost served to warm his room. Plumes of black smoke vied with plumes of grey from the black stacks of the refineries. They burst forth like leaves. These morphed and became birds in the white sky.

He took long walks in the winter landscape to warm himself up and stave off the depression of loneliness. A welcome break from the solitude of his studio.

Finally, in February he collapsed in his bed. He slept for three days. When he emerged, he ate cans of tomato soup he could heat up on the hot plate.

When he got up on the third day he looked around at his work. He had done it. He had painted a whole show. He lined the paintings up around the large room. There were seventeen paintings. Twelve he felt were very nearly great. The largest was 8'x7'. Surrounded by his paintings, he felt like he was in a whole new world. Plants and vines and leaves and trees had climbed and wound all over the cities. Plumes of smoke had morphed into black and white birds. Oceans of sun prism water were crowned by two suns; one red, one yellow. Birds flew in pairs in and out of the painted skies. Since now it was mid-February blue made a crack in the white sky. And just a peek of pink buds were etched out on the tree limbs.

With this fresh burst of spring air, warm change blew in his open windows. He spotted the strong legs running down the sidewalk towards his house. The boy was laughing. His blonde hair grown longer and curly. The woman was pushing the bike and coming playfully along. She was playing catch with him, as the boy hid behind shrubs and then burst forth laughing. When she caught the child up, she stood staring at the house. She looked up at the top floor, staring straight at him. "See," she said, "this is where your grandfather used to live. Long, long, ago. Not now. That was back when he was in college. Before he went on to the rest of his life. We are going to his painting show tomorrow. It's a long trip. We have to go far away to a big Museum in New York City."

But it all started here. He had a room somewhere in that big house. Everything always has to start somewhere. The boy clapped his hands and pointed. He pointed and wiggled and jiggled until she had to put him down. And then they were off again.

❧

THE END

42

TOO EARLY

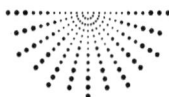

Francine batted her eyes open and saw Johnnies' back to her on the full-size bed they shared. Studying the sculpted form of his biceps and shoulders, she was about to run her fingernail down the length of his spine, when he abruptly got up and left the room. For the bathroom, she supposed. On her knees in bed, she swept her blue paisley dressing gown from the bureau, freshened her lipstick, and fluffed her red hair in the mirror. Twinkly green eyes winked back at her. Before he returned, she lay back down on the bed and feigned sleep watching him thru cracked eyes. He grabbed his pants from the upholstered armchair.

They had a one room sort of place and the bedroom alcove opened up to a sitting room with only chintz draperies separating them. She could see his form in the dusty dawn light that spilled from the large window that overlooked the city and the park. Their place was a small walk up on the third floor, but what a view. The February day seemed to be a grey dismal one.

The smell of old spice flirted with her nostrils as he walked back over to the nightstand. Francine quickly arranged herself on the bed. The gown opened high on her thigh, just showing her satin slip. She extended one slender arm and long finger nailed hand to touch his forearm as he reached for his watch and put it on without so much as a glance in her direction.

This game they were playing was boring. She sat straight up against the headboard, propped up against the lavender scented pillows. She grabbed "The Great Gatsby" and began to read, one leg crossed over the other. The other leg bounced, red toenails pointing. By now Johnnie had his under shirt on. He opened the French patio windows to the smell of diesel fumes below and stepped on to their balcony. His strong lean form filled her with longing as she watched him finally still as he lit up and smoked a cigarette. No matter how many times she felt those muscles under her caress, she wanted more. Her heart lurched at the determined way he sucked on his cigarette. The tip flared orange as he blew white rings that melted into the ash sky. Loss and longing tugged at her. Something was gravely wrong.

She wanted him to stop dressing and come back to bed. He didn't have to work on Sunday anyway. Sunday was their day. The day they slept in. Wrapped into each other with dreams of the night before. Then the two of them would decide together. To prepare bacon and eggs and toast in the small kitchen with the vinyl yellow table and matching chairs, or to just linger over and extra cup of black coffee and then head to the diner on 4th street. She swung her hips as she tiptoed in her bare feet to stand just behind the curtain without stepping outside. The nylon curtain was silky to the touch and she smelled the acrid cigarette smoke hanging suspended at the door. She watched the grey city pigeons fly around in a chaos of wings. A few landed on the balcony rail. Johnnie appeared mesmerized by them. Then she followed his gaze through the narrow city streets to the small park beyond. Church bells began to peal in the distance. Johnnies hand rested on the wrought iron railings. She studied his hand, strong and thick fingered. Veins pulsed with his blood through those warm strong workers hands. The thick gold wedding band was muted gold in the dim light. She should shine it up for him she thought. Of course, he never took it off.

As she watched his hand resting ever so lightly, she knew she wanted those hands right now. Tanned, tender, and so familiar.

She knew what those hands could do to her. And she wanted them. Now. She knew how only he could hold her so tight, right into his heart as if they were one. It was Sunday. Day of rest and timelessness; The day to loose oneself in each other and the Great Creator of the universe. And time stands still. Gravity disappears and you know neither up nor down; The beginning or the end. Floating in the infinity of timelessness and airwaves into nothingness.

She giggled at the thought. Johnny looked straight at her. She turned and walked back towards the bed, sure he would follow. He crushed his cigarette, came back in, closed the window, and turned the lock with a loud click. She cocked her head and looked over her shoulder at him with a slow smile. He looked past her and walked to the flowers, a bunch of virgin white gardenias in a tall oriental vase they had received as a wedding gift. As he bent to smell them, she wanted to kiss the curve of his neck. He strode to the mirror his grim blank stare reflected back. Finally pulling a comb from his back pocket, he smoothed his hair, brushed his teeth, and began putting his shirt on. Francine was mad now.

"Look at me," she screamed. She jumped in front and held his lapels. "Please take this off and come back to bed. It's too early. Too early. Too early. Do you hear?" She sobbed when he completely ignored her and began buttoning his cuffs, and zipping and unzipping his pants to tuck his shirt in properly.

Then he walked out of their beloved one room apartment. Their love nest that had become their dream home- apartment in the city. Later they might have some kids and move to the country but not now. The two of them against the world. She'd left her folks, everything behind for him. Everything was perfect and nothing could go wrong. Love conquers all. And sure, he worked hard at his new business in the city. But money didn't matter, had never mattered.

Where was he going? She hiccupped on her sobs and sniffled to a stop. She ran to the white Frigidaire in the corner. She grasped the thick metal handles and pulled. The inside was bare except for a quart of orange juice and a loaf of Wonder bread. She must have forgotten to shop. She'd missed grocery day somehow. She'd forgotten his favorite foods.

"The way to a man's heart is through his stomach." She sing-songed in her head. No wonder he is mad at me. He didn't look mad. Just determined.

The door opened with a click and she turned to see her Johnnie walk in. He grabbed the clutch of white flowers from the vase. The pungent scent of gardenias followed him out the door. Still not a word. Her heart flew to her throat, a drumbeat in her ears. No words came as her mind spun.

Dejected and alone, she carefully pulled up the chenille bed spread and plumped the pillows. Facing the mirror, she dabbed her green eyes and stood tall. She puffed her hair into place re-inserting the silver combs with care. She found her pumps by the door. She always left them there, eager to get them off as soon as she came in.

Where had that man gone? To get breakfast she realized, he must be starving. She grabbed her trench coat from the coat rack beside the door, pulled the old oak door open, squared her shoulders, cinched the belt tight and headed out. Once Francine reached the street her head darted right and left to spot which way Johnnie had gone. Her eyes blurred again with sadness searching the dimming day.

The church bells chimed again. She counted six loud echoing gongs. Was it already evening? Time was playing tricks on her. He disappeared around the corner and she began to run. She ran and ran, screaming, "Johnnie!" her voice choked and broken as she followed. The darkness swallowed him up.

After she rounded another bend, there he was. Not at a restaurant or diner, he was down at the wharf by the river. Warehouses of sturdy solid old brick lined the cobblestone streets. A mean chill snaked up her legs beneath her coat and the flimsy gown that clung to her calves.

Johnnie stood on the balustrade of the bridge. He gazed out over the river. A few dim stars emerged through the cold steel grey like shark teeth points in the cold air. Evening settled in like an omen. The light from a streetlamp shone on the fragile white bunch still clutched in Johnnie's large hands. Francine wailed again. "No!" He dropped down all at once to the bridge and leaned hard against the railing, burying his whole face in the gardenias. His tears like dew upon the petals.

She screamed, "Johnnie. No."

He turned toward her; his face wet, his eyes streaming. The tender blooms and verdant leaves clashed with his rough stance and broken crumpled form as he knelt on the stone street.

Her lips formed a sad smile beneath the streetlight. Curious, Francine turned and faced the wall. On the spot just over her head, there was a small bronze plaque. She squinted her eyes.

In careful beautifully engraved script, the plaque read:

In loving memory
To my one and only love,
My beloved wife,
Francine.

❦

The End

PART IV- OUR TIME

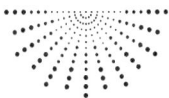

1

OUR MARCH UPON THE EARTH

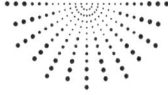

Architecture and poetry clamor
for prominence in a mind
unwilling to define.
To define is to name.
Yet naming is our birth right.

God gave this to Adam.
To name is to have dominion.
The silent stone ruins of the Parthenon,
Or the staid power of Stonehenge speaks

the universal language of form.
The triggered memory in each soul
is like the handing of the baton
in some way to carry on
in our march upon the earth.

Moving rock and erecting form with purpose
In a quiet march of time
of man upon the earth.

*Each civilization is built upon
the ruins of another.*

*In our march upon the earth.
We were here, it seems to say.
We were here.*

2

FUTURE

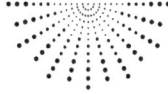

Like a train at full speed going forward
Into the future with no driver.
Machines with no conscious cannot be
Pleaded with, or warned or threatened.
Bribed or manipulated, cajoled or reasoned with.
That is why the roller coaster we are on
That began with the industrial revolution
Fooled us for so long.
We thought we were in charge.
But now we see,
As the loud roar of the inevitable
Pummels us forth into a preordained oblivion.
Like the runaway train.
With no driver.

3
AWAKE

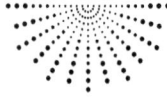

The dark night of the soul
Was on my mind when I found
The painting of the dark Knight,
On a black night
With fireworks exploding
In a New York sky.
Knight of the Night.

I lived in New York once upon a time.
When coffee in blue cups was good
And the twin towers still stood.
When both jewelry and bagels were sold
In the Lower East Side neighborhood.
Galleries full of Old Masters were traded
On the Upper East Side.

Broadway tickets were half price on Tuesdays
And the deli's made lunches
you could eat sprawled on the grass in the park.
The sacred spiral is a code .

The key to architecture and design.
Structures coded like both
plant forms and galaxy.

It's how to make sacred spaces
for everyday folks.
The horse marches majestic.
His erect rider fierce,
With a Horace like beak.
I recall Egypt.
Here the Masonic code was first formed.

Masons schemed inside pyramidal chambers
With rituals of initiation,
The knights Templar invoked.
The Knight of the Night
The dark night of the soul
With massacres and beheadings
Which drove their tribe deep.

Knowledge and wisdom buried lost underground.
The age of darkness hid sages,
healers, and wise woman too.
Purified by fire,
All tried and found wanting.
While Secrets and Truth
Were misunderstood.

Age upon age,
Season upon season
All never repeating
Just spiraling on.
Into new dimensions
The new Aquarian Age
Awake.

Awake to a new dawn bursting with light
From a dark soul night.
Say the Wise Ones

Of the Golden Dawn.

4
SESTINA CONCERNING THE OCEAN

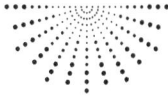

The Poet contemplates the ocean,
After walking long upon the beach.
Why he came here is now forgotten.
As his heart contemplates the sea.
Lost, his walk becomes an invocation,
Pulling sustenance from a hidden place.

Fortune had provided a place
Tucked near to the Atlantic Ocean.
Cold sand gritty of a deserted beach
As night steals the sun he makes an invocation.
Smooth a worn shirt to sit and watch the sea
Rise up in a steel grey light flash. Forgotten

Friends, family and lovers. All forgotten.
Self soon lost to this timeless place.
His heart swam out with the dolphins at sea
He can barely see. Swallowed by the ocean.
Waves, rising high and gliding toward the beach.
Sunsets red-orange glow like a prayer, an invocation.

Energized by answers undeserved to invocations
Unsaid. A melody consumes him words long forgotten.
Seagulls call and flock around landing on the beach.
Drifter like the silver driftwood cast about the place.
Home is found in the multitude of drops within the ocean.
Boats no lost longer call him like a drifter out to sea.

Why do I, while drifting towards the sea,
indulge my dreams in invocation.
Thus invite the longing for the ocean.
Remembering the poet I have never forgotten.
He lives deep within a hidden place
Forever strolling along the beach.

Wind tangled hair, seaweed foam layered beach,
Hands in pockets, the man and the sea.
Regrettably the sea fills the empty place
I'd hoped would make him long for me. Invocation
For loves lost but not forgotten.
The poet who'd held me captive by the ocean.

Lost loves at the beach
Are not forgotten with the smell
Of the sea and a song by the ocean

5
SACRED TIME

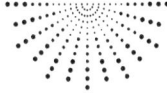

Sacred geometry is the key
to the space time continuum.
The universe forever expanding
in a quest to run from God,
the powerful force of love and light.
The safe place called home.

Home?
As children run away from parents,
to find themselves,
to meet their destiny,
they find a mate.
Some create a life, raise some babes.

One day they look into the face
of their spouse and see their mom.
The world of their youth recreated
in another shock of blue.
Holding hands and spinning in circles
in forevers whirling dance.

I am my Mom and you are my Dad.
How did we repeat the place
from which we both ran?
Worlds within galaxies, galaxies within worlds,
created above and below.
As the familiar repeats itself

and the universe expands.
It's a pattern of repeating geometries
In the space time continuum.
A spiraling energy of change.
Until Now.
The new Atlantis, the Aquarian Age.

6

NEW KING ARTHUR

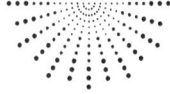

Holy blood, Holy Mary
Arthurian lore
Of Middle Ages turned dark.
The birth of the dark night and the Holy War.

If you happen to be of French descent
and trace your ancestry
to the time of Chartres cathedral,
A seed is already in your soul
with a longing. To go back
to the site of ancient wisdom teachings
brought forth since the time of Christ.
Now they say the new descendant shall be born.
A new King Arthur to lead us on.

7

GHAZAL – ANGEL

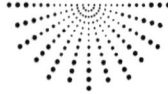

ANGEL

Early morning mists floated
Into my mind like an angel.
The cold night gave way to sun
Understanding dawned like an angel.

Bleak and dark paths lay ahead
I fell on my knees and prayed to my angel.
Stern and fierce with sword in hand
Presence clear no doubt he was the angel.
Mighty forces forge my soul to focus
wrong no hocus-pocus and face my angel.

ONE

As I embrace my angel and hold him strong
I know the desire in me is to be one.

Knowing with surety, Grace and majesty are his alone
as bonds of fear break one by one.

Fear binds me close to earth, when my soul
Desires only to soar and be with the One.

Yet how can a lowly earthling on the 3-D plane ever hope
to mix with mists that blur distinctions and make us one?

So many doctrines, so many men
worshiping so many gods when there is only one.

One true God who bursts all into being.
Hierarchies of angels, God and man all one.

So He says when He proclaims His love
that connects us all and makes us one.

8

PLANES

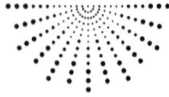

Higher Beings
caught on 3-d planes
Of existence,
Clamor and complain.
While memories of starry worlds
And womb like mother love
Contrast with the shared brittle struggle
Of earthly existence.
Plastic food in plastic places.
Tinny voices on dotty screens.
While illusion makers paste illusion on illusion
And stories told in simple words
Try to paint the truth.

9

ON BEING

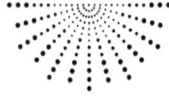

On meaning
Boredom can lull you to sleep.
Don't you see?
The tornadoes and storms
The volcanoes and fires,
Mudslides and rains
The wrong cold
The wrong heat
The lost seasons
Are all there to
Wake us up.

Go to war on hunger and poverty
on lack and shame.
Save the girls from the vampire slave trade
Rescue the children from the drug addicted homes.
We are needed here.
On this war rotten earth.
With poverty stricken values in tinsel town.
We are needed to wake up and serve.

To hold those children
as though they are our children
To love those mothers as Our Mothers
To heal Haitian earth and wind-torn
home less poverty lost ones as though
our very own land and homes were
Falling, falling, falling.
This is Our 3–D world.
Illusion or not
The souls are real
The pain they feel is real.
Those that would care
Are called to
Be present.
Be aware.

Call to action
Call to prayer
Those that meditate open to hear
The voice that calls so loud
Resonant firm, baritone vibration
"Dance unto me.
Wait for my WORD
Do you wait for My world?
Or can you co- create with me?"

THE WORD

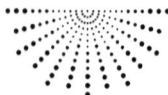

THE WORD

It began with the word.
The whole thing,
The whole story.
The biggest story.
It's all about The Word.
And yet, once everyone climbed the tower of babel,
It's the words, semantics, which tore us all apart.

ONE

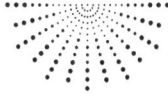

O NE

We all long to be ONE.
Moving in harmony
of wonderfully formed Waves.
Flowing in and out,
Back and forth,
In God's Big Ocean.
Can we hold hands?
As Brothers and Sisters once more?

12

PINION AND THE PINE

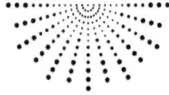

Like a sensitive soul unfurls her wings,
I am emerging.
Looking for a place to soar.
I have loosed my bindings
And let my wings dry
By the river.

I unfurled them in the sun.
They blow in wind and flow
About me. The soft feather touch
Tingling my legs, my arms, my shoulders
Night after moonlit night.
I stand tall beside the pinion and the pine,

As I move up and down the mountain.
Then I lay upon the grass at the feet of Saint Francis
While the wind blows
My wings about me.
I know that soon I shall spread them
Surrounded by freedom's song.

The Spanish aria of deep tones
accompanied by guitar.
My words and drawings are a prayer,
As I watch each star
So that I might see the signs.
Mixed in with the pinion and the pine.

DANCE FLIGHT

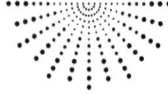

The bonds are tight
My arms squeezing my heart to my chest
As I encircle them around and round and round.
My wings are invisible.
The shredded feathers glued tight,
Cling to my skin,
Wet and wilted and inoperable
Unresponsive to my whim.
My patience has worn thin.

Somehow fate showed up.
Seraphine carried me away.
She drove me to Taos at midnight.
Enveloped in stars I could touch.
I stood on tiptoe
I began to dance.

Somehow with my pounding feet upon the earth,
My arms begin to loosen
From the tight binds of my chest.

My heart grew two sizes as it filled with air.
Breathe, breathe, breathe, they said.
Get your buried head out.
Turn your face to the mountains,
Look to the sun.

For days I pounded my feet into the earth
While my face looked up.
The purple mountain stood silent
While my laments and my fears
Pounded rain upon the mesa.
A mesa of cacti and tears.
My hair and my feathers hung limp with sweat.
I swayed to and fro with the dance.
Dance light and fleet of foot
I dance swirling, whirling, wind blue
The lightning sparked.
I flew.

1 4

TAOS DANCE

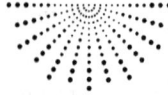

I flew.
I touched the night sky.
With my breast bared and facing up
I arched everything I had back.
The light of the multitudes pierced me.
And I let it soak in.
The light like seeds in my soul,
Once planted took root.

As each morning I awoke
I placed one foot at a time
Upon the bare wood floor.
Step by step
I moved to steady pulse of dream beats.
The wood warming my soul.
Step. Beat. Leap.
My speed increased.
My skirts encircled bare legs

Freedom and laughter

Followed behind.
Chasing me round the room.
A happy warmth caught up with me
Joy leaped with me as smoothly I floated
around and around
over and through.

15
PAIN

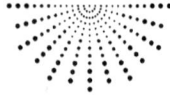

Pain sharp and fierce
Wrenched my heart and squeezed.
I couldn't breathe.
Choking on silent screams
Wrapped in barbs of a tenacious vine.
Vines grown entangled in my skin and hair,

I couldn't think.
My mind emptied
Into my pounding feet and walking stick.
I danced with it.
It became first staff then arrow,
Then sword, then wand.
I needed magic to release the bond.
Reaching for love beyond,
Warrior Nicole helped severe the ties.
I longed for Dance and flight.

Wilted, ragged, sweaty, and sore,
A worn twisted up rag of a doll.

And then I saw the feathers fall.

Feathers in cascades of turquoise and blue,
Purple, pink, and green serene.

I found myself
I found my voice
I knew my name.
And then with one great leap
Toward purple mountains
I flew.

To move. To run.
Dance - skip - leap
The spiral of ascension
Created in grace.
One transcendent leap to new dimensions.

The place of peace
Once sought now found.
Pain washed clean by colored rain.
Reborn on the feathered breasts of angels.

16
WRAPPED IN EGYPT

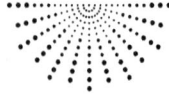

Wrapped in Egypt and dreams
I began to write
once more.
The muse had been silent
Leaving me to wander
Nature's path.

And nature's gifts
Have now adorned me.
The sun, golden in its rise,
Awakened me to write.
It is time to tell the story.
Wrapped in the cocoon of night.

I had been dreaming.
Now, fully awake I embrace
The chrysalis of morning.
The birds' song layered, one on top the other,
Like a chaos of sound, when
All the instruments tune up at once.

Distant trees, their silhouettes etched in lazy dawn,
Maple trees that guard my dwelling,
Cannot stop the sun's rays from piercing through.
It is the light—
no matter the private darkness of my heart
That beckons me forth

To greet the day
Once more.

CHAPTER EIGHTEEN

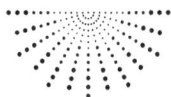

ACKNOWLEDGMENTS

I am grateful and owe a huge debt to mentors that opened the world of poetry to me. Most especially Jeff Hardin and Bill Brown. I also found a deep resonance with the universal Christian Philosophy of Kahlil Gibran and Mary Elizabeth Haskell whose life and work further encouraged my writing journey.

ALSO BY MICHELLE MORACZEWSKI

'Pink Expressions', Watercolor, by M.Moraczewski